Contents

Preface	01
Using this Book	01
A Word about Colour	03
Getting Ready	07
Understanding the Ingredients	09
• *The Dyes*	09
• *Soda Ash*	10
• *Salt*	11
• *Water*	12
Preparing & Arranging the Cloth	13
• *Manipulating wet vs dry*	14
• *Artful Scrumpling*	15
• *Pleating*	15
• *Spirals/Chelsea Buns*	17
Making & Applying the Dyes	18
• *Dye Recipes*	18 & 19
• *General approaches for applying the dyes*	20
• *Starting Off; using a single colour*	21
• *Moving On; using 2 primary colours*	21
• *Taking Off; using 3 primary colours*	22
• *Murking it Up; creating & using complex colours*	23
Dyeing Threads	25
Rinsing the Dyed Cloth	26
Going Further - Projects to Explore	27
• *Three + One*	27
• *Stack & Seep*	29
• *Natural Elements*	30
• *Using the Leftovers*	37
Over-Dyeing for Richness & Depth	39
Troubleshooting	43
Resources	44
Further Reading	45

Preface

Cloth is tactile, cloth is fl[...]
used. If the cloth doesn'[...]
provides a creative outpu[...] As such
our students, fellow textile artists and friends generate and use
cloth for quilts, stitched textiles, textile art, clothing, soft furnishings,
interior design, accessories, sculpture and even jewellery.

We formed Committed to Cloth in 2000 as a result of a
shared love of textiles - we're both practising artists who also
love to teach. One of our key goals is to provide the best tutors
in professional, spacious studio environments – but you can find
out more about that on the web site. Our skill base and
experience spans wet work (dyeing, screen printing etc.), dry work
(stitch, construction, textile art etc.) and personal development
(composition and design, personal imagery, feedback and critique).

We want people to learn, develop, grow and most importantly,
enjoy their work with cloth and stitch.

Using This Book

So what is Tray-Dyeing? Essentially it involves packing cloth into a
tray of any size, pouring over single or multiple colours of dye and
leaving it to work its magic. The resulting cloth is glorious in texture
and colour. The marks achieved from various forms of manipulation
are always fascinating and can range from being graphically crisp and
detailed to soft-focus, haloed and gentle. The colour combinations
and palettes can range from the serene to the downright bizarre.

How then should you use this book? Any way you like, although
we've tried to structure things in a way that builds knowledge,
experience and ultimately, understanding. As such, we'd
recommend you work in a fairly step-by-step manner. However,
we do appreciate that people learn in different ways so if you
want to, jump around in any way you like! Whatever you do, work
consciously, pay attention to what's happening in front of your
eyes, take notes if it helps and above all, take risks. And if things
don't work out, try to figure out why and just do them again.

We identify strongly with the words of John Holt, an influential
educator: "We learn by doing. There is no other way". It's all about
process so we'd encourage you to get stuck in, give it a go, pay
attention, experiment, explore and play. Accept that you won't fall
in love with every piece of cloth you generate and remember with
some further effort, you can often change the 'dogs' to superstars!

Tray Dyeing | 01

Leslie had fun with scraps of hand-dyed cloth in a type-tray, embellishing with threads

A Word about Colour

Before we got stuck in to the main topic we thought it would be worth providing a few points about colour. Most people love colour and yet many are afraid of playing with it, perhaps believing it's an ability you're born with. Well okay, some people do have a greater affinity with colour than others but there are things you can do to develop ability;

- paying attention is a key element – looking at nature, conscious play and experimentation with dyes, examining the colours created when they're mixed and the way the proportions of the different colours affect the end result.

- having a dialogue about colour with yourself and others. When Leslie moved from Africa to England in the mid-eighties, she was blown away by the different colours in the landscape. She and Ann Wilson would go for walks and take turns to provide detailed descriptions of the colours they were seeing. If you do this alone or with a friend it'll help you to develop your own personal vocabulary of colour. Nancy Crow and Kaffe Fassett are masters of colour and their books are worth reading for both the pictures and the way they talk about colour.

But where to start? Let's take a look at the basic terminology…

Colour is the property of light, not a thing in itself and the order of the rainbow spectrum is always the same;

Violet
Indigo
Blue
Green
Yellow
Orange
Red

So there we have it, a rainbow lighting up the sky. Let's dig a bit deeper…

- *Hue;* is a property of colour, for example a particular shade of Red. Hue is simply the name of a colour and describes the visual sensation of the different parts of the colour spectrum. One hue can be varied to produce many colours for example; pink, rose, scarlet, maroon, crimson. Each is a colour but the hue in every case is Red.

- *Value;* refers to the lightness or darkness of a hue. When mixing colours, value can be altered by adding white or black to the colour. Adding white produces a tint, adding black produces a shade. White dye doesn't exist so to create values we use smaller amounts of dye or dilute the dye mixture to produce a paler value of any given colour.

- *Intensity;* refers to the brightness of colour, sometimes called saturation of colour. The intensity of a colour can be lowered by mixing it with small amounts of grey or the complementary colour (the colour directly opposite on the colour wheel). So to reduce the intensity of Red you could mix it with a drop of Green.

Colour Schemes & Harmonies
Many colour schemes and harmonies exist but for the purposes of this book, we felt it would be helpful to cover three key schemes;

- **Monochromatic;** involves the use of only one hue which can vary in value and be used in conjunction with pure black or pure white.

A monochromatic colour scheme using Scarlet & Magenta. There'll be lots of tonal variety once the cloth has been rinsed and dried

- **Analogous;** combines several hues sitting next to one another on the colour wheel, for example Yellow, Orange and Red. The hues may vary in value from light to dark.
- **Complementary;** complementary colour schemes join colours opposite each other on the colour wheel, producing a 'shock' factor through the sense of contrast. For example Red and its opposite, Green; Yellow and its opposite, Purple; Blue and it's opposite, Orange.

A complementary colour scheme of Golden Yellow and Purple

Tray Dyeing | 03

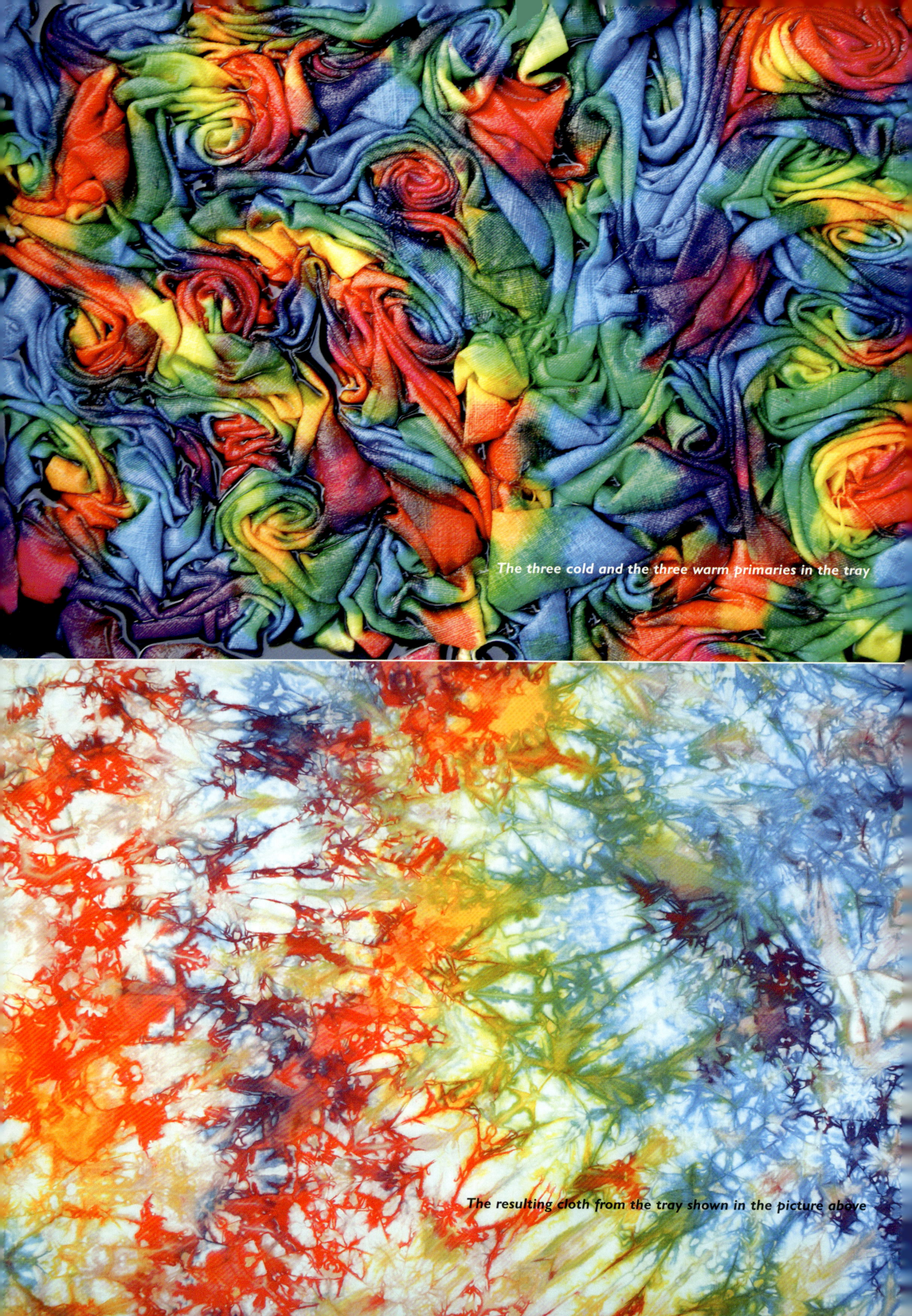

The three cold and the three warm primaries in the tray

The resulting cloth from the tray shown in the picture above

A colour-wheel made from magazine cut-outs

The Organisation of Colour

The most common organisation for the relationship of the basic colours is found in the colour wheel, which classifies 12 hues divided into three categories;

3 Primaries	Red, Yellow & Blue
3 Secondaries	Orange (Red & Yellow)
	Green (Yellow & Blue)
	Violet/Purple (Blue & Red)
6 Tertiaries	These are mixtures of a primary and an adjacent secondary; blue and green generate Blue-Green; red & violet generate Red-Violet and so forth.

Cold & Warm Primaries

You may have heard people who are involved with dyeing talk about 'cold and warm' primaries. So what are they…

Cold Primaries	Warm Primaries
These are high energy, bright and 'sparky'	These are low notes, muted, rich and subtle
Lemon Yellow	Golden Yellow
Magenta	Scarlet
Turquoise	Mixing/Royal Blue

The results you'll get when mixing cold colours together vs warm colours will be quite different. For example;

Cold mixes;
- Lemon Yellow & Magenta will give you a bright, brilliant, 'acid' orange.
- Lemon Yellow and Turquoise will make a brilliant, sparky emerald green.
- Turquoise & Magenta will give you a bright, sparky purple.

Warm mixes;
- Golden Yellow & Scarlet will give you a warm, rich orange.
- Golden Yellow & Royal Blue will give you a dirty green… not quite olive, but almost.
- Royal Blue & Scarlet will give you a plummy purple.

The three warm and three cold primaries

Tray Dyeing | 05

The Cloth

Mx Dyes are formatted for use with cotton, linen, hemp, silk and viscose/rayon. They will not work on synthetic fibres such as nylon or polyester, nor are they effective with wool – even though wool is a natural fibre. Cellulose fibres such as cotton, linen, hemp and viscose/rayon will take a dye colour differently to protein fibres such as silk. In addition, different fabrics generate a different 'strike' or colour take-up.

Every type of cloth is different; some have fine fibres and others have heavy/thick fibres. Some are tightly woven whilst others have a loose weave structure. Let's take a brief look at this…

Fine vs thick fibres; the Mx dye will react in the fibres once soda ash/sodium carbonate is added to the dye bath or is present in the cloth (more on this later). Any type of individual fibre is only capable of holding so much dye – a fine fibre will hold less dye and saturate more quickly, a thick fibre will hold more dye and take longer to saturate. Jane Dunnewold suggests imagining the cloth as a car park capable of holding a finite number of cars. When the car park has reached its full capacity, no more cars (dye molecules) will be able to get in – the fibre will be fully saturated. To allow more cars in, you'd have to drive some out through a colour removal or discharge process. So, a very fine Silk Pongee/Habotai is a smaller car park than a heavy cotton velvet one and less dye will be needed to fill up the silk than the cotton.

Weave structure; a tightly woven fabric will mean that the dyes have to work harder to get inside the fibres. A loosely woven fabric will be easier for the dyes to penetrate. Imagine different types of fencing; an open trellis will allow the elements through easily whereas a densely woven fence will make it harder for the wind and rain to penetrate. It's the same with a weave structure and what you're working with will have an impact on the crispness of the marks achieved.

Note; we personally avoid using muslin or other 'loomstate' fabrics for anything other than high-water immersion dyeing as it's so resistant to dyes. If you choose to use muslin or loomstate for the projects in this book, scour it very, very well and accept that it will take many processes and perseverance to get a decent depth of colour – but when you do get it, it can be fabulously rich.

As you work with dyes and different fabrics, it's always worth experimenting and making some (rough) notes on the differences in dye strikes and colours. This means you'll be able to prepare dye baths and dye paints that are right for the cloth and the colour saturation you're looking for… and you'll waste less dye because your quantities will be more accurate.

Light-weights and heavier weights

Different weave structures in the cloth

Washing/Scouring the Cloth

Whilst some cloth is supplied 'PFD' (meaning it's prepared for dyeing), others may not be, particularly if bought from retailers or market stalls etc. It's important that any fabric you use is pre-washed to remove size as it can prevent the dyes from penetrating the fibres. The easiest method is to simply pre-wash your fabric at 60° C. Consider washing it twice if you feel that it may have a lot of size in it.

To guarantee removal of size, it helps to scour fabric in a rinsing agent such as Synthrapol SP/Metapex 38 and soda ash/sodium carbonate. Textile rinsing agents are designed to remove size from fabric or catch up, hold and remove excess dye from fabric. For scouring with a rinsing agent and Soda Ash, wash the fabric as follows:

- Load fabric into washing machine (don't over-fill)
- Sprinkle in 3 tablespoons of Soda Ash and 1 teaspoon of rinsing agent for a full load of fabric (about 6 metres). The amount depends on the type of fabric – a fine silk will need less soda ash and rinsing agent than a heavy-weight cotton or velvet.
- Wash at 60° C.
- Any shrinkage will also occur at this stage, which is useful.

The same colours will strike differently on different fibres

Understanding the Ingredients

The Tray-Dyeing Process

When you use dyes in a bucket (high-water immersion) the dye swirls around in the solution and finds its own way in to the fibres – it's not being applied directly on to the surface of the cloth. When dyeing in a tray (low-water immersion) the dye solutions are applied to the cloth in a very direct and specific way – you're placing them where you want them. We therefore consider tray-dyeing to be a 'direct surface application' process. So, although the ingredients are the same for both approaches, the recipes vary slightly as the application method is different.

There can be a lot of mystery surrounding the use of Procion-type Fibre-reactive Mx dyes and the whole dyeing process itself but in truth, you don't need to be a chemist or a rocket scientist to get great results. We believe that if you can learn the function – or role – of the different ingredients used it will help you to make sense of the process, develop an intuitive approach and give you the confidence to seek the colours and textures you want. Plus, other books and recipes will have context which will make them easier to understand and use. With a little thought and lots of conscious play and experimentation, you'll soon develop an approach that suits you.

The Role of Urea

We mention Urea here because even though we don't use it for immersion/tray dyeing it's commonly used in other recipes. Urea is a 'hydroscopic' or wetting agent meaning that it constantly attracts moisture to itself from the atmosphere. Its role is to keep things wet (which is why it's used in the base solution for dye paints) and it can sometimes be useful to have around to help dissolve stubborn dyes. However, we find that a bit of warmth and manual aggression – good stirring or shaking the solution in a sealed container – does the trick!

The Role of the Dye

The Mx dyes are your colouring agents (sorry to be obvious!). They're fibre-reactive and used in conjunction with Soda Ash, the chemical used to drive the reaction between the dye and the fibre. They're at their most dangerous to health when in their dry/powder state so wear a good quality mask when mixing significant quantities. Equally, wear gloves when handling the dyes and if they do get on your skin, don't use bleach to remove them. Instead, use a cleaner such as Reduran to get the worst off - the stains will fade after a couple of days.

Mx dyes are classified as 'cold water' dyes but in fact, they're made to be used at a temperature of somewhere between 50-70°C. Icy cold water straight from the tap or boiling water from the kettle needs to be avoided. If using the dyes as paints, the heat element of the process is provided during the setting or curing/batching process whilst when working with salt-based dyeing, it's provided through the use of warm-to-hot water.

Once mixed as a warm/hot solution with salt, Mx dyes can be stored for a limited period of about 3 days but if the solution has had soda ash added to it, the shelf life is between 1-3 hours. Be aware that if you use an old (no soda) dye solution it will have gone cold and the dyes will therefore be 'sluggish' and not strike as well. DO NOT warm them up in a microwave! Instead, consider one of two options;

- use them cold and accept that the strike may not be as good due to the dyes being 'sluggish'
- warm them up by adding hot water and accept you're diluting the strength of the mixture when using them in a tray.

We source our dyes from Kemtex Educational Supplies and the list below shows the names and numbers as used by Kemtex at the time of writing. As a colour range we recommend two sets of basic primaries; 3 cold and 3 warm. Black and Dark Brown have been included to use as colours in their own right or to help you generate 'murky/complex' colours and darken/enrich the primaries;

Warm Primaries	Cold Primaries
Scarlet Red Mx-3G	Magenta Red Mx-8B
Royal Blue Mx-R	Bright Turquoise Mx-G
Golden Yellow Mx-3R	Acid Lemon Mx-8G

Good 'Mixers'/'Murking' Colours are;
Black Mx-K and Dark Brown Mx-3G

Dissolving soda ash/sodium carbonate

Feel free to invest in a larger colour range – we do! Other good Kemtex colours include;

- Indigo Navy Mx-2G; a useful dark blue
- Red-Brown Mx-5BR; tea-rose in colour, Red-Brown is great for warming up Golden Yellow or enriching both Magenta and Scarlet
- Olive Green Mx-G; a useful 'dirty' green
- Rust Orange (from the 'CD' range); not too dirty, this is a good 'warmer'
- Petrol Green (from the CD range); an attractive blue-green/green blue – depending on your perspective!

Many dye manufacturers produce pre-mixed colours that are 'pale' tints of something stronger, e.g. Pale Aqua is often drawn from something like Petrol Green. Think carefully before investing in these pale colours as they are often a poor economy. You can find pale tints by either mixing much smaller amounts of dye or by using semi-exhausted dye solutions. Save your money and invest in colours that can be very difficult to find when you're starting out – such as neutrals.

How much dye to use is a tricky subject, mainly because it's subjective and it's important to note that some colours 'strike' faster and take more aggressively than others. We'll be more specific about dye quantities and mixing in the 'Making & Applying the Dyes' section.

The Role of Soda Ash/Sodium Carbonate

Soda Ash or Sodium Carbonate is the chemical fixative needed to generate the chemical reaction with the dyes and fix them into the cloth. If soda ash is added to the dye solution it has an active life of about 1 to 3 hours and cannot be stored for later use.

Preparing the soda solution

Tray-dyeing involves putting the soda ash into the cloth rather than putting it into the dye solution. As such it's a good idea to mix a stock solution and keep it in a lidded bucket. It doesn't go off and as long as it's kept covered it won't evaporate.

Wear a mask when mixing significant quantities of soda solution as the dry fine particles are hazardous if inhaled. Soda Ash doesn't like being dissolved in hot water, so start by putting the required amount of soda ash in a bucket and add enough tepid water from the tap to get it dissolving. Then, top up with the required amount of either hot or cold water. The quantity of soda ash increases if large amounts of dye are used but the basic recipe for a soda soaking solution is;

- **3 tablespoons of soda per litre of water.**
- We always keep a large stock of soda solution on the go, dissolving 450ml of soda ash into 10 litres of warm water. A 5 litre stock bucket is probably more realistic for home-dyeing so dissolve 225ml of soda ash into 5 litres of water.
- When we want to add soda ash to the dye solution (which we do for high-water immersion dyeing) use 3 tablespoons for up to 3 teaspoons of dye (our 'standard' strength 99% of the time). However, if we're using a dye solution that's more than 3 teaspoons of dye (which can happen when bucket dyeing), we double the amount of soda to 6 tablespoons dissolved in the bucket to which the dyes will be added.

Don't skimp on soda, it's important to the process!

The Role of Salt

We choose to use salt when immersion/tray dyeing as it makes the dye solution more efficient. Many dye processes ignore this cheap yet efficient chemical, but we use it as it helps the fibres of the cloth to relax and encourages/speeds up the penetration of the dye into the fibres. There are two things to remember when calculating salt;

- *the amount of salt in the dye solution is proportionate to the amount of dye you're using. You'll use more dye for stronger, more saturated colour and therefore more salt in the dye solution.*
- *salt amounts are not proportionate to the amount/volume of water (more on water levels in a minute).*

We always make a 'strong' strength solution of salt water and dilute it accordingly. We find that the salt dissolves much more easily if it's mixed with boiling water in 1 litre containers. As we mix, we decant into a bucket, which has a lid to prevent evaporation.

But what if you don't want a dye strength that calls for a strong-strength salt solution? Easy…

- if the amount of dye we're using doesn't call for such a strong salt solution as we have in our salt bucket we simply use less of it, e.g. we'll take 500ml of our strong salt solution and top this up with 500ml of hot water – in a flash we've diluted the strength of the salt solution by half.
- the added bonus to this approach means that if our salt solution gets cold (which it does when we make it in advance), it's easy to heat it up again using this method.

For tray-dyeing here's how we use our salt solution in relation to dye quantities.

Strength	Salt Solution
'Strong' 2 teaspoons of dye	1 litre of strong/full strength (200ml salt) salt solution
'Medium' 1 teaspoon of dye	500ml of strong salt solution (a 1/2 portion)
'Weak' 1/2 teaspoon of dye	250ml of strong salt solution (a 1/4 portion)

Whilst simplistic in approach, we know this method works well for tray dyeing as the dyes are directly applied on to the cloth as opposed to reaching the cloth by swirling around in a bucket. When bucket (or high-water immersion) dyeing we alter the salt and dye quantities somewhat and this is covered in the 'Over-Dyeing' section of the book.

We've tested dyeing with and without salt and in our minds, there's no question that salt makes a difference to getting a decent strike. As salt is cheaper than dye, we choose to use it.

Tray Dyeing | 11

The Role of Water
Water (moisture) is a key ingredient in the dyeing process. The two key things to bear in mind are the volume and the temperature.

Water Volumes
The volume or amount of water used in the vat/tray will help to determine the texture of the dyed cloth. A lot of water (high-water immersion) helps to achieve a smooth, even finish – although stirring the vat/bucket is also important to encourage the dye to spread itself evenly through the cloth/fibres. Low-water or 'tray' dyeing generates a more textured result as less water is used, the dyes are directly applied on to the surface of the cloth and there's no stirring (we do meddle a little, but more on this later).

Water Temperature
Although Mx dye is labelled as a 'cold water' dye this simply means it doesn't need to reach boiling temperature. The label 'cold water' tends to be used to differentiate Mx from other dyes such as Direct Dyes and Acid Dyes, which do require a boiling temperature.

Mx dye doesn't actually like cold water, preferring the water to be between 50-70°C. Heat helps the fibres of the cloth to stay relaxed, speeds up the absorption of the dye into the fibres and speeds up the fixing/the setting time. The result? Greater take-up of dyes and less waste. However, don't use boiling or very hot water as if the temperature is too high it may split mixed colours. But, there's no need to get the thermometer out. As a general rule of thumb if the water is steaming or feels uncomfortably hot through your gloved hands, it's too hot so let it cool down a bit before using it.

Quilt artist Jette Clover noticed a marked difference in the depth of colour she was getting in her hand-dyed cloth once she moved from Northern Europe to Florida. She put this down to the significant increase in ambient air temperature – her dye baths stayed warm and as such, generated a better strike.

And just to make you feel better, even Nancy Crow struggled with her dyeing. She writes: ('Nancy Crow', Breckling Press, 2006)…

"I'd had such bad luck with my dyeing during the cold months… and was beginning to think I did not know how to dye my RICH colours. But as the weather warmed up I discovered two things – room temperature in my dye room needed to be 70°F minimum – it had been too cold for the dyes to set. AND I was not using enough dye per yard nor enough soda ash to fix the dyes. Ann Johnston helped me with this when I showed her my ugly results – washed-out, grayish colours."

So, if you've been using cold water from the tap to mix your dyes you should notice a much better result once you switch to using warm-to-hot water.

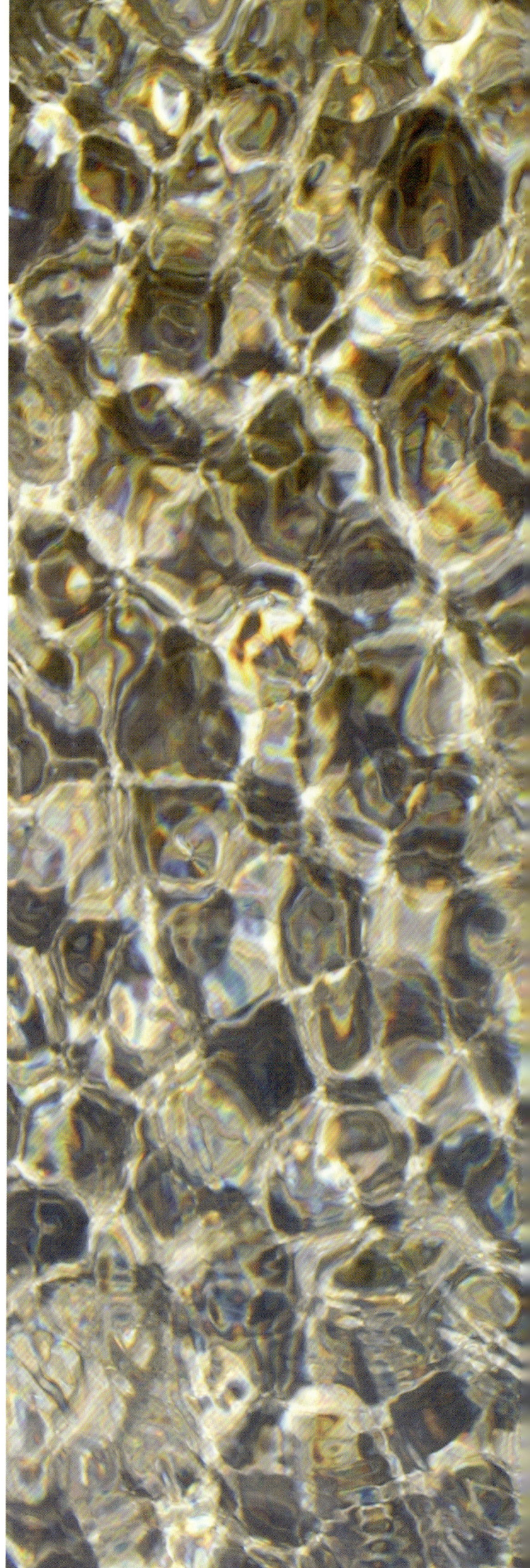

Preparing & Arranging the Cloth

There are many ways to manipulate cloth to get textural marks — but we decided to stick to three key methods rather than write a book about Shibori!

Start by choosing a tray size appropriate to the amount of fabric you're going to manipulate and dye. It's a bit difficult to say how much cloth you can get into a particular size of tray but generally speaking;

- For lots of texture, think lots of compaction — the cloth needs to fit very, very snugly in the tray. Leslie manages to get 5 to 9 metres of fabric into a 3'x3' seed tray (more than enough for a queen-sized quilt-back), and over 1 metre of a medium-weight cloth into a small 'kitten litter' tray.

- For less defined marks think less or looser compaction. The fabric is still arranged 'artfully' but across a larger surface area. So, instead of compacting 5-9 metres of fabric into a 3'x3' seed tray, Leslie might only arrange 3 metres, spreading it out across the tray.

When dyeing with several colours, the secret of avoiding results that have 'mud' in them lies in tight compaction — the colours are applied directly where you want them and start striking immediately as the cloth has soda ash in it. Tight compaction means that the colours don't move around and blend easily — colours strike where they hit on the surface of the cloth. Eventually they will of course seep down through the compacted cloth on to the bottom of the tray where they will form 'dregs'. These 'dregs' will simply add a darker, crisper texture to one side of the fabric.

Tightly-compacted cloth; combining pleats and scrumples in the same tray

Scrumpled cloth that's been less tightly compacted

You can just see the 'dregs' sitting on the bottom of the tray

Tray Dyeing | 13

Cloth that has been manipulated dry getting it's bath of soda ash solution. The tray will be drained after 10-20 minutes

Lifting cloth out of the soda ash solution

Arranging wet, soda-soaked cloth in the tray

Getting the soda solution into the cloth

Tray-dyeing works best when the fabric has been soaked in soda and used wet. Dry fabrics tend to resist the dyes. Getting the soda ash solution on to the cloth means the cloth will be wet and relaxed before the dye solution is added. This means that as soon as the dye hits the cloth, it'll be easier for it to penetrate and it'll start to strike and fix straight away. Remember that the basic recipe for your soda ash stock pot is *3 tablespoons of soda per litre of water*. All you then do is let your fabric soak in the solution for 10-20 minutes.

You can soda soak before arranging your cloth in the tray, or after. Let's look at both options.

Manipulating Dry cloth

Manipulating dry fabric will generate crisper – even mathematical – results (dare we suggest such a thing!) But, it's generally more difficult to arrange dry fabric as it doesn't want to stay put and springs out of place. Ironing it into place helps and you can use clamps or elastic bands if you want to (although we don't). Spirals are deep and crisp if done with dry cloth and finer and more irregular with wet cloth. If you do arrange your cloth dry, once it's in the tray pour warm/hot soda solution over it – making sure the fabric is covered. Leave it soaking for 10-20 minutes and place another tray on top as a 'catcher' or lid, press down, tilt and drain the excess soda back into the soda stock bucket.

Manipulating Wet Cloth

Wet fabric is easier to manipulate than dry as it tends to stay put. Wet manipulation will generate finer, more irregular marks with interesting areas of bleed or halos. To arrange wet fabric, simply place your cloth into your soda ash stock pot. Leave it for about 10-20 minutes and then squeeze out the excess soda (wear gloves) before arranging it in the tray.

As we're going for tons of texture, whether you manipulate the fabric wet or dry it must have soda in it before the dye is applied. This means that as soon as the dyes hit the cloth they'll start to strike immediately as they work their way down, around and into the hills and valleys.

Let's now take a look at three key ways of arranging the cloth – whether it's wet or dry.

Artful Scrumpling

Artful scrumpling creates scrunchy texture, flower and leaf shapes, skeletal, x-ray and crystalline marks, strange beasts, insects and even faces. Scrumpling works best with wet cloth, so soda-soak it first and arrange it as follows;

- Lay down a sheet of plastic on to your bench/table – big enough to hold the wet cloth. Place your tray at one end/side.
- Squeeze out the soda-soaked cloth and place it on the plastic behind or to one side of the tray. Very wet, drippy cloth will give different results to cloth that's been wrung out more thoroughly, so experiment with this.
- Gradually draw the wet cloth in to the tray, artfully scrumpling it into hills and valleys, lumps and bumps and scrumply bits.
- This takes time so work slow and work steady. Keep tight, keep compacted and pay attention to the edges of the cloth.
- Try to generate an even amount of texture on the bottom of the tray as on the surface.
- Don't worry if some of the tray is empty – it's better for the cloth to be tightly compacted than too loosely arranged.
- Avoid leaving big bubbles of cloth poking out.
- Drain off any excess soda solution.

It's now time to apply the dye(s) which is covered in the next section, 'Making & Applying the Dyes'.

Scrumpling wet, soda-soaked cloth. In this instance the tray is almost full, but don't worry if it isn't!

A close-up of scrumpled cloth, ready to dye

Scrumpled cloth manipulation creates great texture – these marks are quite crystalline

Pleating

Pleating the wet cloth creates lines, ripples, 'watery' marks, trees and grasses. Before you start, choose a tray that's the approximate selvedge-to-selvedge width of the fabric, or cut/tear the fabric down to a size that fits the long side of the tray. Again, this is a technique that works best with wet cloth, so pre-soak your fabric in the soda solution first, then…

- Lay down a large sheet of thick plastic on to your bench/table, and place your tray at one end.
- Lift your cloth out of the soda bucket, squeeze out the excess soda (but keep things pretty wet) and cascade the cloth on to the plastic behind the tray.
- Draw it in to the front of the tray and keep drawing in, pleating it into ripples as you go.
- Work slow and work steady. Keep tight, keep compacted… but DON'T worry about getting your pleats even (this is not a book requiring precision skills). If you want precise, even pleats, we suggest you iron your pleats into dried cloth, lay it in the tray, pour on soda and then drain after 20 minutes.
- Don't worry if some of the tray is left empty – it's better for the cloth to be tightly pleated/compacted than too loosely arranged.
- Variations can be achieved by altering the sequence to interrupt the pleats, you can move the pleats diagonally to create a change of direction or you can manipulate curves into a 'snake' of pleated cloth.
- Drain off any excess soda solution and move on to apply the dyes (see next section).

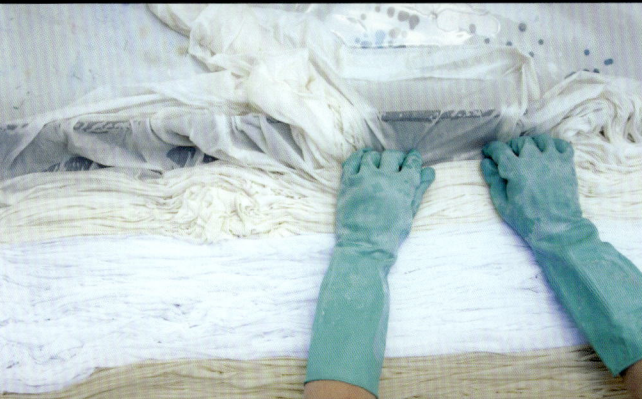

Pleating wet, soda-soaked fabric in a rectangular gravel/seed tray

Tray Dyeing | 15

A silk Habotai scarf tray-dyed by Jan Wise - brilliant!

Twirling a spiral on a silk-viscose velvet scarf

An arrangement of spirals in linen

Spirals/Chelsea Buns
Twirling the cloth in to curved, pleated lines will create spiral shapes or ammonite-like marks. This can be done wet or dry to achieve a different look each time.

- Lay the wet (soda soaked) cloth (or T-Shirt or scarf) out on to plastic or a smooth, even surface.
- Take a spoon (wooden or metal) or spatula and place it on the cloth - where precisely will depend on how many spiral shapes you want to generate. If you're working on a T-Shirt, beware of creating a target dead-centre in the chest or 'spiral breasts' that may cause unwanted attention!
- Start turning the spoon/spatula – the cloth will start coming together in a spiral form. You may have to help things along a little with some pleating/curving assistance. Do this as many times as you need/want to.
- Once you're done, slide a rigid piece of plastic under the cloth, lift it up and slide it in to a tray. Re-arrange/tidy up if necessary.
- If you've decided to manipulate with dry cloth, try to work directly in the tray as moving dry twirled cloth can be difficult. Add the soda ash solution to the 'dry spirals' and drain it off after 10- 20 minutes.
- Time to apply the dye(s).

So, we've covered Scrumpling, Pleating and Spirals/Chelsea Buns. These three approaches aren't exhaustive, so do experiment with your own methods of arranging the cloth.

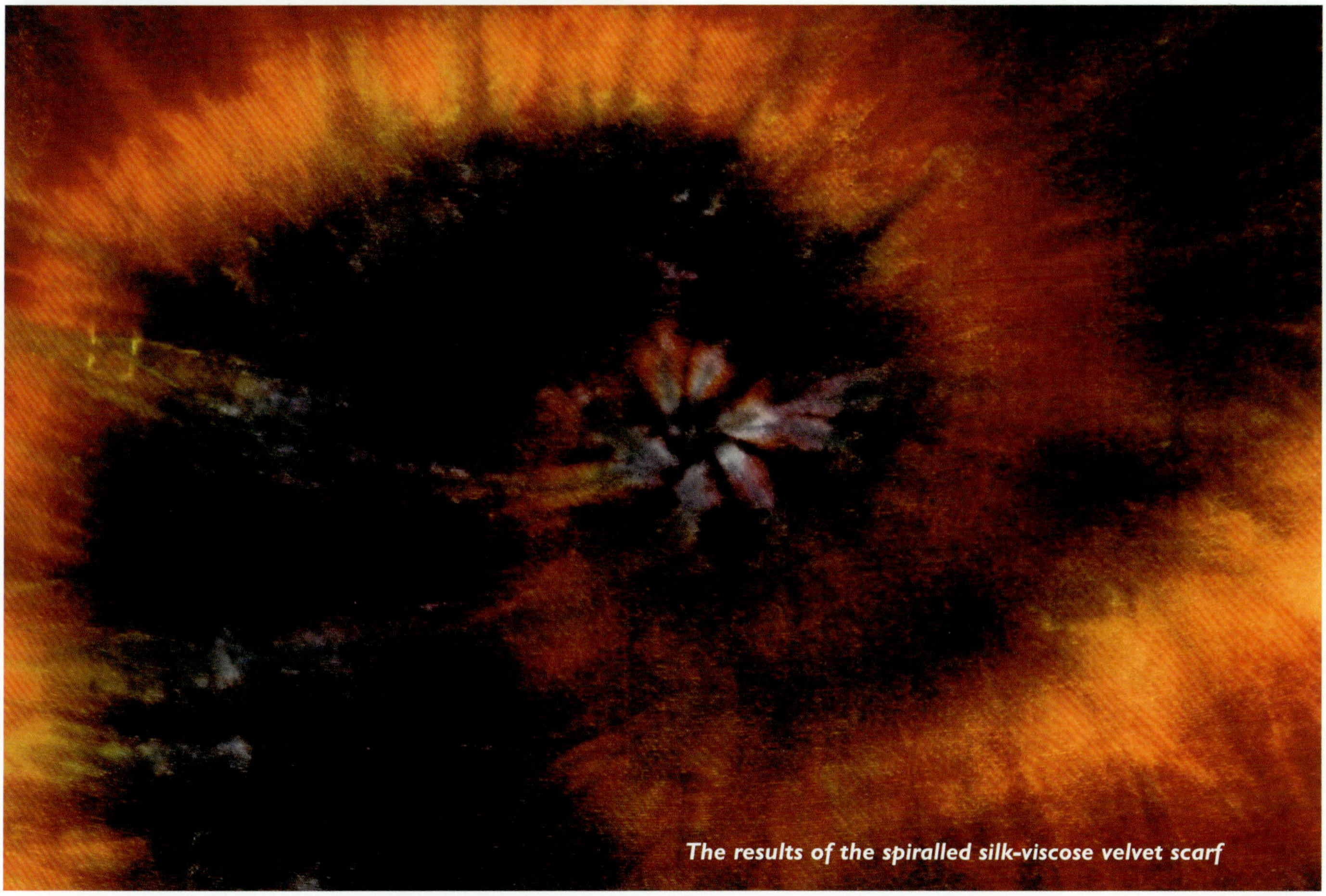

The results of the spiralled silk-viscose velvet scarf

Tray Dyeing | 17

Making & Applying the Dye

Making the Dye Solutions

Writing recipes is always a tricky subject whether it's for dye solutions, French Dressing or Spaghetti Bolognese! How much dye to use is a very subjective - what we might classify as a pale colour could be very different to what you classify as a pale colour! We're not precise, accurate souls either. We don't weigh our cloth to decide on dye quantities, preferring to make decisions based on;

- the type of cloth we're using, e.g. fine silk vs heavy linen
- the weave structure (tightly or loosely woven)
- the amount (yardage) of cloth we're using e.g. a quarter metre or 3 metres
- the strength or depth of colour we want

The table below shows the recipe we use when tray-dyeing. It demonstrates how we adjust the amount of salt according to the amount of dye we're using. It will make 1 litre of dye solution - how much cloth that will dye and how deep the colour is will depend on the cloth, e.g. fine silks vs heavy linen.

We never go below a half-teaspoon when tray-dyeing and recommend that you undertake the exercises and projects in this book by using the strength shown in the middle row of the chart: 1 teaspoon of dye. This will usually generate a good depth of colour on the equivalent of a metre of standard-weight cotton.

- *For fine-weight fabrics or when seeking pale colours, use the bottom row of the chart.*
- *For heavy-weight fabrics or when seeking strong colours, use the top row of the chart.*

Dye Amount	Salt Solution
2 teaspoons of dye	1 litre of strong/full strength (200ml salt) salt solution
1 teaspoon of dye	500ml of strong salt solution (a 1/2 portion), topped up with 500ml (a 1/2 portion) of hot water
1/2 teaspoon of dye	250ml of strong salt solution (a 1/4 portion), topped up with 500ml (a 3/4 portion) of hot water

At times you may not need a full litre of dye solution (e.g. if using small amounts of cloth). If this is the case, simply make 500ml of solution and reduce the dye and salt amounts proportionately. This is simplistic in approach but we know it works well for tray dyeing as the dyes are directly applied on to the cloth, as opposed to reaching the cloth by swirling around in a bucket. When bucket (or high-water immersion) dyeing we alter the salt and dye quantities somewhat and this is covered in the 'Over-Dyeing' section of the book.

Let's just underline that when we measure, we're not accurate - never running a knife across the top of the teaspoon. In fact because some dye colours 'strike' faster and take more aggressively than others, we often use 'skinny' or 'fat' teaspoon measures;

- **Magenta and Scarlet** are the 'hares' and 'bullies' in the race to occupy fibre space and as such, we often mix them a fraction weaker – a 'skinny' teaspoon.
- Whilst **Acid Lemon and Golden Yellow** are pretty quick to strike they're easily bullied out of their true nature by all of the other colours. As such, we tend to mix both yellows to a 'fat' teaspoon measure – sometimes up to 50% stronger.
- **Blues and Blacks** can be slow to strike and grab their space in the fibre (the tortoises) but they do get there. Turquoise can be particularly lazy so we often use a 'fat' teaspoon measure for turquoise.

As you use the dyes you'll discover their characteristics and develop your own way of measuring - just as we tend to compensate with our 'skinny' and 'fat' teaspoons.

Let's get mixing ⟶

- Let's assume you have a strong (200ml to 1 litre of water) salt solution already prepared.
- Take a 1 litre container and put in a little warm/hot (but not boiling) water.
- Measure in the appropriate amount of dye powder (we're suggesting 1 teaspoon for now) and stir until it's well dissolved. Some dyes dissolve better than others so if you're having problems with lumps, either use pots with screw on lids and shake the solution vigorously, or dissolve a small amount (1 tsp) of urea into the water first to help the dye dissolve.

- Having dissolved the dye, add 500ml of strong salt solution, stir and then...

- Top up to one litre with hot (but not boiling) water, stirring and checking for un-dissolved dye. If you get lumps, strain the dye mixture through a dedicated tea strainer.

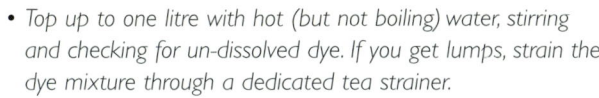

Tray Dyeing | 19

Applying the Dyes

Your wet, soda'd cloth is in its tray. Your dye is mixed. There are two basic techniques when it comes to applying the dye(s);

1. **On top/through the surface;** this technique involves 'basting' or squirting the dye mixture fairly evenly over the top of the manipulated cloth until the whole surface is covered. We use a turkey baster (large pipette) or a squeeze bottle as both give good control, but you could also use a small jug. To control the drip factor with a baster/large pipette, put your gloved finger over the end of the nozzle as you lift it out of the dye pot and release it when you get to the target area. The aim of this approach is cloth that has very little white left in it, so we always make sure the dye penetrates thoroughly and will often massage the surface of the cloth; patting/stroking the dye down into the layers. Massaging can be done as you apply the dyes or 15 minutes later.

2. **Flooding;** this technique involves pouring the dye into an empty area of the tray, or slowly down one corner of the tray. The solution seeps and runs along the bottom of the tray – flooding it. Keep adding dye until the level reaches at least half way up the cloth and tilt the tray to encourage flooding. Colour will 'wick' up the fabric from the bottom of the tray. The aim of this approach is to leave plenty of white/un-dyed areas or areas of very pale colours where the dye hasn't managed to wick up through the compacted cloth. As such, don't massage or meddle!

You can try these approaches separately or combine them both in the tray for varied effects.

So, what about the colours you'll use? A key thing to remember is that if you use more than one colour of dye when dyeing in the tray, the direct surface application across the surface of the cloth means that the 'pure' colours will strike where they hit. Eventually they'll mingle and create new colours – particularly on the bottom of the tray. This means that one side of the fabric will have darker, crisper marks as a result of sitting in the dregs.

But, all of this means you need to think carefully about the colour combinations you're going to use and the kind of colour you're going to get when they meet each other and intermingle. Because of this conundrum we've chosen to take you though a step-by-step colour-approach - starting cautiously and ending adventurously - but you can of course start any place you like…

Put your finger over the nozzle of the baster/pipette until you reach the target zone

'Flooding' Scarlet dye down the side of the tray

Applying Acid Lemon dye to the surface of the cloth after the Scarlet had been 'flooded' in

Cloth that has been tray-dyed in Black using just the 'flooding' application method

20 | Tray Dyeing

Starting Off – Using a Single Colour

This first level starts you off with a single colour of your choice. This will help you to understand the basics of the process and how texture is generated as a result of the dye finding its way through the manipulated cloth - without any colour scheme distractions. The result will be a tonal or value study in the chosen colour, giving a monochromatic result. This may vary if the dye powder/colour decides to split but this phenomenon tends to only happen in composite or mixed colours such as black, brown, rust-orange and so forth.

Golden Yellow being poured over the surface of the scrumpled cloth

Magenta & turquoise dyes applied in rows

Golden Yellow dye has been applied. Now it's time for the second primary – Royal Blue

- Cover your bench with plastic if it's not already covered, and lay down a drop cloth on the floor if you're prone to spillages.
- Assemble your tray of arranged/manipulated soda-soaked cloth, your dye solution and a turkey baster (or decant your dye solution into a jug or squeeze bottle).
- Apply the dye solution by basting it on to the surface of the cloth in rows, curves, squiggles, chevrons, plaids etc. Wait for 15 minutes and then massage the cloth slightly. Or…
- Flood the dye solution in by pouring it into an empty area of the tray or down the side of the tray. Let the solution seep and run along the bottom of the tray (tilt the tray to help things along) and keep adding dye until the level reaches at least half way up the cloth. Colour will 'wick' up the fabric from the bottom of the tray. Don't massage or meddle.
- Once the dye has been applied, leave the tray for at least 4 hours. To extract maximum colour strike, leave the tray for 12 hours, or even overnight. The more exhausted the dye, the easier the rinsing and the more efficient you're being with your dye stocks.

Moving On – Using 2 Primary Colours

This second level takes you to using two primaries of your choice. This will help you to understand how they mix and intermingle and what secondaries they produce. Exactly what you'll get will depend on the proportions of the primaries used, how they're applied, how they move through the cloth and how they mingle in the bottom of the tray, so experiment. Let's assume that…

- You've covered your bench with plastic and put a drop cloth on the floor if you're prone to spillages.
- Your trays of arranged/manipulated cloth are ready along with two (labelled) pots of your chosen dye colours and two turkey basters - or decant your dyes into jugs or squeeze bottles (also labelled).

When applying the dyes, remember to pour or baste on the colours slowly and steadily and in a way that allows the dye to flow through the fibres to the bottom of the tray. Experiment with;
- applying the dyes in rows, plaids or chevrons.
- applying the dyes in swirls, radiating lines or randomly across the surface of the cloth.
- applying the dyes at opposite ends of the tray and allowing them to blend where they meet in the middle (tip the tray to encourage this).
- applying them in an unbalanced way – more of one colour than the other – which will produce unbalanced secondaries such as reddy-oranges etc.
- mixing different strengths of primaries where one is weaker than the other.
- mix a secondary colour from some of both primaries. Apply both primaries but leave some areas white. Then apply your mixed secondary to the white areas, massaging the cloth to blend and avoid hard lines.

You can also mix unbalanced secondaries that don't have equal proportions of both primaries in them. The end result of unbalanced mixing is always subjective to the proportions you use but a good starting place is to try using a ratio of 2:1; this is a big enough jump in the proportions to produce (for instance) a yellowy-green or a bluey-green.

3 warm primaries; Golden Yellow, Royal Blue and now Scarlet

You can just make out the dregs in the bottom of the tray. Darker, crisper marks will be generated on the cloth by these dregs in addition to the pure primaries

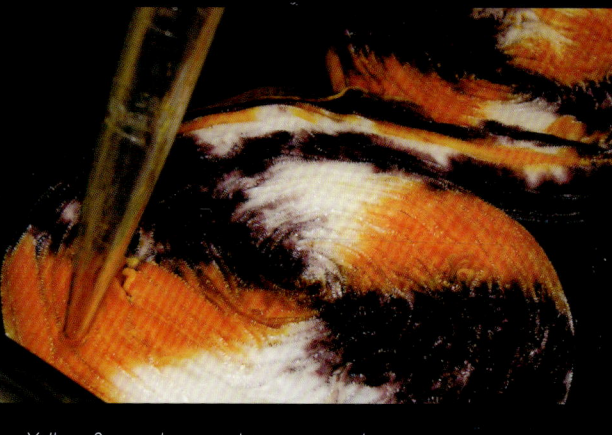

Yellow & purple; complementary colours

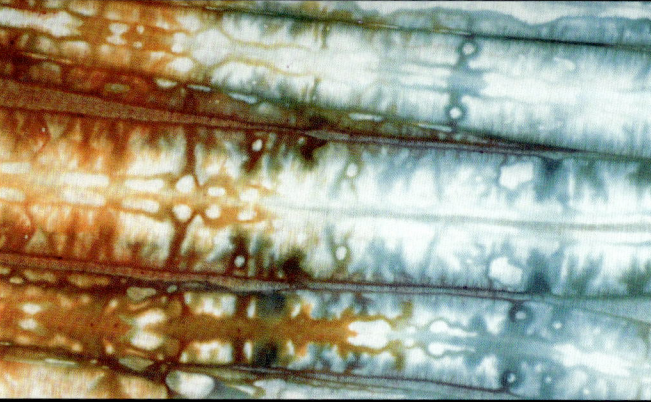

The results of using the complementary colours of Rust Orange and Petrol Blue. Great texture too

Taking Off – Using 3 Primary Colours

This third level takes you to using three primaries of your choice (cold, warm or a combination). Using three cold primaries will produce a range of colours that are fresher, perkier and brighter than when using the warm primaries. Either way, sooner or later you'll be generating some form of brown depending on how things meet and mingle. So, let's assume that…

- You've covered your bench with plastic and put a drop cloth on the floor if you're prone to spillages.
- Your tray of arranged/manipulated cloth is on the bench.
- You've mixed three primary colours; the volume required for each colour will depend on how much cloth you're dyeing. 1 litre of each colour may be too much so consider mixing a half litre of each colour (1/2 tsp of dye to 250ml of cold salt solution and 250ml of hot water).
- Label each colour as it can be easy to confuse them.
- Three turkey basters are at the ready - 1 per pot of dye. Or, decant the dyes into jugs or squeeze bottles (label them if this is the case).
- Apply the dyes…

- How and where you apply them will make a difference to the end result, so experiment with both organised and organic/chaotic methods of application. Try not to 'dot' the colours about in an erratic and superficial manner on the surface of the cloth as this will result in a 'spotty' insipid effect.
- Try applying two of the dye colours on the surface of the arranged cloth and flood the third dye colour in along the bottom of the tray.
- Work slowly and steadily and make sure the colour penetrates the cloth well and flows into the fibres.
- Let the tray sit for a minimum of 4 hours to fix.

Once you've got used to using all three primaries, consider moving on to experiment with other colour combinations…

Analogous
Three colours close to each other on the colour wheel will provide a blended colour scheme with no unpleasant shocks. Try;
- both Yellows and both Blues, and a Green
- both Reds, both Yellows and an Orange
- both Reds, both Blues and a Purple
- substituting one colour with a 'variant' such as Blue Violet, Petrol Green, Indigo Navy, and Cerulean Blue etc.

Complementary
Try playing with various complementary colour schemes;
- Red and Green; choose whether to use Magenta or Scarlet as your red. Think about what kind of green would work best with the chosen red and mix it accordingly.
- Yellow & Purple; choose whether to use Acid Lemon or Golden Yellow. Think about what kind of purple would work best with the chosen yellow and mix it accordingly.
- Blue and Orange; choose whether to use Turquoise or Royal as your blue. Think about what kind of orange would work best with the chosen blue and mix it accordingly.

Remember, where things meet and blend will generate some kind of brown, terracotta, murky brick or even chestnut.

Murking it Up

Here we'd like to suggest experiments with murky or complex colours that are 'off' their true nature. This includes colours that have a small portion of their complementary colour in them, or colours that have been altered by adding small amounts of black or dark brown. For example, ochre, rust orange, olive green, petrol green, midnight blue, tan, aubergine and so forth.

The use of the complementaries to create create complex colours is a key mixing principle. So, to 'murk up' Golden Yellow into Ochre you would use the complementary colour of yellow which is some kind of purple. As you have two reds and two blues in your colour wheel to make that Purple there's room to experiment. You could also choose to use Brown, but that'll limit the type of Ochre you get, so try both options;

- mix different purples by using different combinations and proportions of reds and blues. Add them bit by bit to your Golden Yellow to find out the different kinds of ochre they generate.
- Mix some Dark Brown dye and add that bit by bit to your Golden Yellow and see what kind of Ochre that generates.

When mixing complex colours, the end result is always subjective to the proportions you use so try the following approaches for complex secondaries;

- start with a secondary that is mixed from 1 part each (equal proportions) of two primaries and a half-part of the complementary to produce - for instance - an Olive Green or Terracotta. Or…
- mix the secondary using equal parts of the primaries required and then add the complementary colour bit-by-bit until you get the exact shade of complex colour you want.

These different approaches will produce a never-ending range of complex colours and that's the magic of it all! Here are some suggestions to play with;

- **Rust Orange;** the complementary of Orange is Blue so to generate a Rust Orange you'll need to mix an orange and then add blue to it bit by bit. Try equal parts of Golden Yellow & Scarlet to make the Orange and then add approximately a half part of Turquoise (or for a different rust orange, substitute Turquoise for Royal Blue).
- **Olive Green;** the complementary of Green is Red so to generate Olive Green you'll need to mix a green and then add some red to it. Try mixing equal parts Golden Yellow and Royal Blue and then add (up to a half part) Magenta or Scarlet.
- **Chestnut Brown;** 1 part Golden Yellow, half parts each of Scarlet and Royal.
- **Petrol Green;** 1 part Turquoise with a smidge of Black and a smidge of Acid Lemon (experiment with your 'smidge' amounts!)

We also use Black & Brown as agents for generating dark, rich colour effects. We use Black as the darkening agent for blues and reds and Brown as the darkening agent for yellows and reds. We make this decision based on the fact that the Kenactive Black dye we use has a blue undertone. If it's used with the yellows, you'll get greens - great greens but certainly not ochre! If it's used to darken magenta you'll get a pinkish maroon whilst if you darken magenta with brown you will get a deep, rich, brown'ish magenta. Try the following mixes;

- **Rich Claret;** 2 parts Scarlet, 1 part Magenta, a half part of Black. Or, try 2 parts Magenta, 1 part Scarlet and a half part of black (fiddle with the proportions of black).
- **Blood;** try 2 parts Scarlet, 1 part Magenta and up to 1 part Dark Brown.
- **Dried Blood;** try 2 parts Scarlet, 2 parts Dark Brown. You may want to add some Magenta.
- **Aubergine;** try 2 parts Scarlet, 1 part Magenta, a half part Dark Brown and a half part Black (and try switching the Scarlet and Magenta proportions and fiddling with the Black and Brown proportions).

Complex colours

A selection of colours that have been darkened using either Black or Brown

Tray Dyeing | 23

The permutations are infinite and fiddling with the proportions is one of life's great joys! Ultimately it's important to remember that we all see and describe colours differently. The kind of terracotta, olive, aubergine, ruby, chestnut, ochre, rust orange, plum that you're seeking will be different to someone else's. As such, you need to experiment with proportions until you get the colour you want. Having got it – make a note of how you got it or commit it to memory. Or just have fun trying to find it again!

When applying complex dye colour schemes some sort of order will prevent too much chaos and result in cloth that has a logic to the movement of colour within it. Chaos might be what you're looking for if you intend to cut the cloth up or use it as background for further wet work. Rhythm might be the desirable outcome if you want to use the cloth in larger pieces as background for appliqué, embroidery or garment yardage. When using a wide range of colours we usually apply the bright, pure hues first so that as the other colours are added, the 'base' or 'under' colour gleams through the subsequent layers. So, consider trying:

- darkening the outer edges of the arranged cloth with black, brown or a complex colour mixture.
- adding structure on the surface of the cloth with accents of black or brown once the initial 'pure' colour has been applied.
- flood in black or brown by applying it into an empty area of the tray and letting it run along the bottom until the level reaches at least half way up the arranged cloth. Tilting the tray helps with the distribution. Then, baste the brighter colours in patterns on the surface of the cloth. Try this in reverse as the effect will differ.

So, what's left…

Darkening the edges of the cloth using brown dye

Adding structure or accents by applying black dye to the surface of the arranged cloth

Dyeing Threads

It can be great fun to dye threads, lace and tape in the tray at the same time you dye your cloth, particularly when using two or more colours. If you do choose to dye threads, there are two key principles to consider;

- Make sure that your thread is well-hanked and secured with four figure-of-eight loose ties.
- Threads often have a great deal of size or dressing on them and this needs to be removed before dyeing. To remove size, simply put your hanked threads in some hot soda solution - use the same recipe given on page 11 - and let them sit for 30 minutes before lifting them out and squeezing out the excess soda.

Arranging the Threads

We recommend placing the hanks of thread on top of your arranged cloth. This will produce a strong, defined result and achieve a true 'variegated' look when several colours are used. Having arranged your cloth, simply arranged your soda-soaked threads on top and then apply your dyes in the usual manner.

Initially, the threads will stop the dyes from getting to the cloth so once they're saturated with dye solution, lift the threads out and place them in another tray to fix. Then, continue applying dye to the cloth in the tray.

Having left the threads to fix or set for a minimum of 4 hours, rinse them. Don't rinse your threads with your fabric – an unholy tangle will ensue! Instead, lift them out of the tray, cup them in your hands and give them a quick rinse under running cold water or put them in a small bucket and swoosh them around a bit. Then, put a couple of drops of rinsing agent in a small tub, top up with hot water, add your threads and let them soak for between 30 minutes and 3 hours. Some threads can be stubborn, so you'll need to experiment. Finally, do a couple of cold water rinses and hang them up to dry.

If the variegated effect is too strong for your liking, you can of course over-dye the threads.

Secure your hanks of thread using a figure-of-eight tie

A selection of threads, lace and tape on top of the arranged cloth in the tray

Dyed threads sitting on top of the cloth

Drain the (exhausted) dye solution out of the tray

Run cold water over the tray and drain again

Transfer the cloth to the sink or a bucket

Rinse, rinse, rinse! Change the water regularly

Rinsing the Dyed Cloth

And now for some donkey work! Your trays have been sitting quietly for between 4 and 24 hours. It's time to rinse them out to stabilise the cloth and get rid of any excess dye.

Rinsing your cloth well is important – particularly if you're piecing something like a quilt. Washing a quilt that's been made from different coloured hand-dyes that subsequently bleeds can be disastrous! Even if the cloth is being used for something that won't be washed it's important to get rid of excess dye as any remaining traces can oxidise over time.

We generally use a rinsing agent such as Synthrapol or Metapex 38 that's been designed to;

- encourage loose dye particles out of the cloth.
- trap and suspend loose dye particles and avoid back-staining.

Rinsing agents create foam so be cautious with them. A half teaspoon is enough for a full machine load, so reduce the amount appropriately. If you don't have a specialist rinsing agent, use something that's suitable for woollens or delicates.

To rinse;

- Pick up the tray and drain off the left-over dye solution.
- Then, run cold water over the cloth in the tray and drain again. If you're using a large gravel tray be careful it doesn't twist or tilt suddenly and spill.
- Now transfer out the cloth from the tray and place it in the sink or a bucket.
- Using cold water (and ideally, a few drops of rinsing agent), keep rinsing and changing the water until it runs clear(ish).
- If rinsing same or similar colours, machine wash at 60°C with some rinsing agent. If you've gone for strong, dark colours do this twice.
- If you're rinsing multi-coloured cloth or cloth from different trays together, machine wash cold with some rinsing agent and then machine wash at 60°C to get rid of any final loose dye traces.

Note; consider putting a piece of un-dyed cloth into your first machine wash – it's often possible to get a delicate, pale tint from the excess dyes coming out of the tray-dyed cloth.

26 | Tray Dyeing

Going Further - Projects to Explore

If you've had a go at everything we've suggested, you should have a pretty good grasp of tray dyeing by now. The possibilities are endless and we encourage you to explore, take risks and venture in to the unknown. However, we know this can be scary so here are some themed projects to consider. We also recommend sending your cloth through any given project twice to generate true richness and intensity.

Making a Gradation
Some of the projects in this section call for several strengths of the same colour – a gradation. As such, we thought it would be useful to cover the basics of making a gradation of dyes where the basic approach is to mix a dark- strength dye solution and then cut it down by adding warm water.

- Have ready a litre of warm, strong salt solution (200ml of salt dissolved in one litre of water).
- Mix a strong strength dye solution using 2 teaspoons of dye, dissolved in a little warm water and topped up to one litre with the strong salt solution. Stir well and label this pot 'Dark'.
- Now tip half of this 'dark' dye stock into a second, one litre container and top up with warm water. Stir well. You have now reduced the strength of the dye (and salt) down by 50% or half. Label this pot 'Medium'.
- Now tip half of this Medium strength solution into a third one litre container and top up with warm water. You have now reduced the strength of the dye (and salt) down by 75% to a quarter strength. Label this pot 'Pale'.

You can dilute the dye stocks endlessly but for the purposes of the projects we're sticking to 3 simple values; dark, medium and pale. So, you should end up with a half-litre of dark strength and a litre each of medium and pale.

On to the projects…

Three + One
On page 22 we explored using 3 primary colours in the same tray and we now suggest you explore even more complex colour schemes. The fourth colour will potentially add more complexity, more contrast or more richness depending on your choice of colour.

This is a tricky project to explain so here are some examples;
- *3 Primaries;* if you've mixed 3 cold primaries (magenta, acid lemon and turquoise) consider making the fourth colour one of the warm primaries (scarlet, golden yellow or royal blue). Or you may have mixed 3 warm primaries in which case, make the fourth colour any one of the cold primaries.
- *3 Secondaries;* if you've mixed 3 secondaries (orange, purple and green) pick one of the primaries used in mixing them as the fourth colour.
- *Any 3;* for any combination of 3 colours consider using Kenactive Black or Dark Brown as the fourth colour.
- *Variable Strengths;* try mixing 3 colours to a pale strength and the fourth colour in a strong strength.

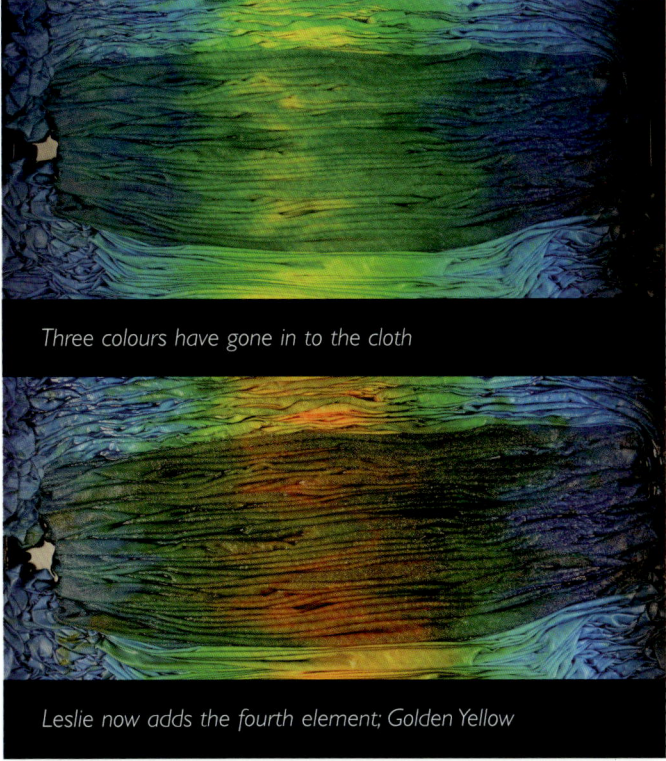

Three colours have gone in to the cloth

Leslie now adds the fourth element; Golden Yellow

So, let's proceed…
- To begin, soda-soak and arrange the cloth the way you want it in the tray.
- Now mix 3 'main' colours in any strength or combination of strengths you wish.
- Apply the 3 main dye colour solutions any way you want to.
- Apply the fourth colour. Consider the following;

- If you've chosen to use 3 primaries, apply the fourth primary (which will be the opposite – warm vs cold - of your original three) on top of its 'mate' in the tray. For example if you've mixed a warm Golden Yellow as the fourth colour to go with your three cold primaries, put that Golden Yellow where you've applied the cold Lemon Yellow.
- If you've chosen three secondaries, add the fourth primary colour to the secondary on the cloth that contains it. For example, if one of your original three was an Olive Green made from mixing Royal Blue, Golden Yellow and a Scarlet, choose either Royal Blue or Golden Yellow as the fourth colour and apply it on top of the Olive Green. An alternative to this is to use a different blue to the one you used for making the Olive Green – such as Turquoise… and so on. Endless variations on a theme.
- If you've mixed a range of pale-strength colours with the fourth colour being a dark strength, apply the pale colours evenly across the tray/cloth, then either apply the fourth dark colour on the surface of the cloth in a manner that creates accents, or flood the bottom of the tray with it.

Let the tray sit for a minimum of 4 hours and then rinse and wash as usual.

Tray Dyeing | 27

The results of the 'Stack & Seep' project. The bottom piece of cloth was the one in the bottom of the tray

Golden Yellow and Purple dyes being applied on the surface of two layers of scrumpled cloth for the 'Stack & Seep' approach

Look at the seepage – the level of the dyes is slowly rising up the container

The final dribble of Golden Yellow goes in to the 'Stack & Seep' container

Stack & Seep

This approach involves stacking two layers of cloth – one on top of the other in the tray.

- Arrange two layers of wet, soda-soaked cloth in the tray – one on top of the other (scrumpling is the easiest way forward with this project).
- Mix two dye solutions of the same strength in colours of your choice (try a complementary colour scheme).
- Pour them in columns on to the surface of the cloth; alternating between each colour.
- Then, pour each colour down the side of the tray to flood the bottom.
- Wait 15 minutes then press both layers of cloth down into the dye.
- Let the tray sit for a minimum of 4 hours and then rinse and wash as usual.

A view of the top layer of the 'Stack & Seep' container. Well saturated!

Tray Dyeing | 29

An effect referencing 'dead' grasses. A touch of Golden Yellow has been added to the basic colour scheme of Acid Lemon and Brown

The same 'dead grass' piece of cloth having been tray-dyed twice using the same colours as before.

Grasses

- Choose cloth that will fit into the width of one of your trays (too big a tray is fine) or if you only have small trays, cut/tear the cloth to fit the width.
- Take some soda-soaked fabric, lift it out of the bucket and use dripping wet.
- Pleat the cloth as described on page 15.
- Mix the dyes as shown to achieve different effects;

Effect	Dye Colour(s)	Strength
Lush Grasses	Turquoise	Mix each dye to a a Medium strength
	Royal Blue	
	Acid Lemon	
	Golden Yellow	
	Black	
Dead Grasses	Dark Brown	3 strengths; Dark, Medium & Pale
	Acid Lemon	Pale

- Apply the dyes using the following variations;

- Lush grasses; apply and massage in both of the yellows along the 'grain' of the pleats/grasses, saturating the whole cloth and leaving no white. Then apply both blues in specific random areas to create variegated effects. Wait 15 minutes and then flood the base of the tray with the black dye. Do not press the cloth down into the tray.

- Dead grasses; apply and massage in the pale and medium strengths of brown dye. Then dribble on and massage in the acid lemon in small amounts along the surface of the pleats. Wait 15 minutes and then flood the base of the tray with the dark-strength brown dye. Do not press the cloth down into the tray. (Note; to experiment, try flooding the base of the tray with black dye as well as dark brown).

- Let the tray sit for a minimum of 4 hours and then rinse and wash as usual.

32 | Tray Dyeing

Applying the dyes in serpentine waves for the 'Monet' effect

'Monet' water

Water

- Choose cloth that will fit into the width of one of your trays (a too-large tray is fine) or if you only have small trays, cut/tear the cloth to fit the width.
- Take some soda-soaked fabric, lift it out of the bucket and use dripping wet.
- Pleat the cloth as outlined on page 15 and try some 'imperfect' pleating with uneven slips, lumps and bumps to create turbulent water.
- Mix the dyes as shown below to experiment with the effect you want;

Effect	Dye Colour(s)	Strength
Caribbean	Turquoise	Mix both dyes to a Medium strength
	Royal Blue	
Monet water garden	Turquoise	Medium
	Royal Blue	Medium
	Aqua (1 part Turquoise to 1/4 part Acid Lemon)	Pale
Moonlight water	Black	Medium strength

- Apply the dyes;

- Caribbean; apply the dyes in ripples and waves along the pleats, but not across them. As you apply the dyes, massage the area where the colours meet to blend them. Make sure the fabric is totally saturated, although leaving areas of white between the pleats can give a sense of light on the water.
- Monet; apply the dyes in serpentine waves across the whole length of the pleats, crossing the colours. Massage after 15 minutes.
- Moonlight water; apply the black dye in ripples and waves along the pleats, but not across them. Do not saturate the cloth – leave ripple areas of white to create a sense of light on the water and don't massage the colour in.

- Let the tray(s) sit for a minimum of 4 hours and then rinse and wash as usual.

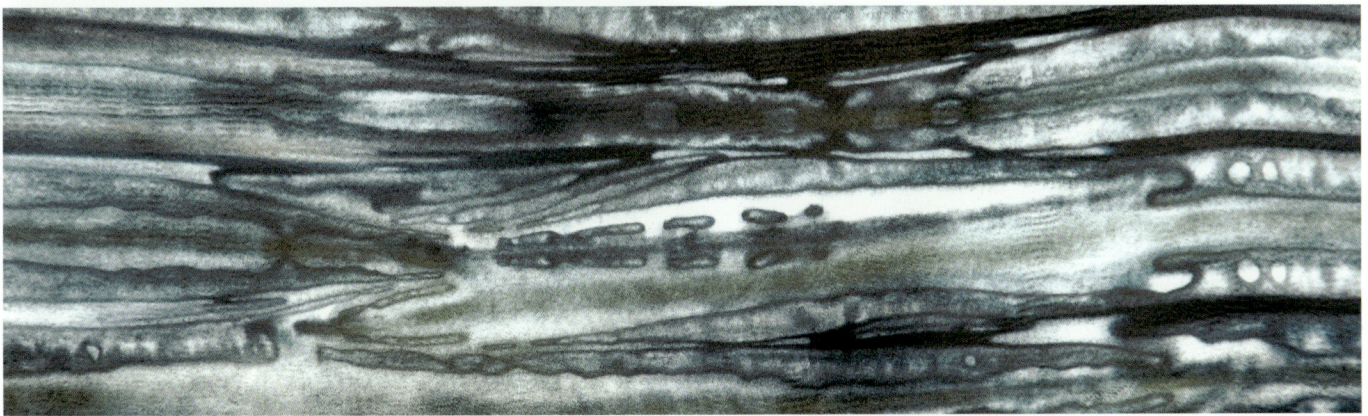

The centre section of the landscape effect. Think abstract!

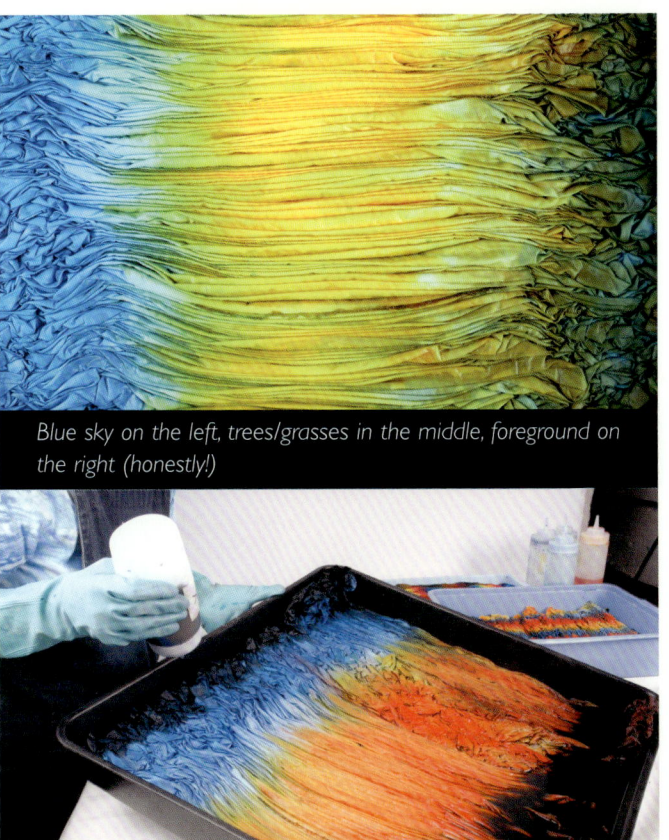

Blue sky on the left, trees/grasses in the middle, foreground on the right (honestly!)

'Flooding' Scarlet dye into the tray to deepen the mood and add accents of new colours

Landscapes

This approach creates a landscape effect of tree trunks, foliage/sky and foreground. You can decide which season your landscape falls into by choosing appropriate colours, for example;

- a spring or summer landscape is likely to need both Royal Blue & Turquoise to create a brighter sky.
- an autumnal or winter landscape is likely to use some Turquoise, plenty of Royal and some black to make things moodier.
- a scarlet is going to be necessary to create trees and a murkier foreground suggestive of autumn.

We suggest you start by mixing all of your dyes to the same strength – Medium. With later experiments you can reduce or increase the strength of any of the colours to achieve different effects. At the end of the day don't get too literal about your landscapes – think abstract, think impressionistic, think Monet!

So, let's get going...

1. Choose cloth that is wider than the width of the tray.
2. Take some soda-soaked fabric and lift it out of the bucket and use it dripping wet.
3. Pleat the cloth in an imperfect manner across the centre section of the tray to create tree trunks. Scrumple the cloth at each end of the tray; one end will be tree foliage and sky, the other will be foreground.
4. Begin by applying blue dye to one area of scrumpled fabric; this will be your starter for the sky. Saturate this area and massage the dyes in.
5. Now dribble and massage in yellow(s) across the pleats in the centre of the tray and the scrumples at the bottom end of the tray. This will start the process for the tree trunks and the foreground. Massage the yellow(s) in down the tree trunks. Press down the yellow(s) in the scrumpled area.
6. Now add a different blue to the top scrumples (sky end) to make it richer/more varied.
7. Now add a lot of blue to the bottom scrumples to create the green for the foreground and stroke it up into the tree trunks to green them up a little.
8. Now flood blue and black into the sky end of the tray to beef it up. Tilt the tray to send this mixture down the tree trunks and provide texture.
9. Now apply red to the bottom (foreground) scrumples – use quite a lot to generate plenty of brown (dead bracken!). Then tilt the tray towards the sky end to flood some red into the tree trunks to give them added texture.
10. Let the tray(s) sit for a minimum of 4 hours and then rinse and wash as usual.

Just experiment with your colours and consider trying out weird combinations - you don't have to be literal!

Tray Dyeing | 35

This piece of cloth has been re-dyed in the tray using old, cold left-over dyes and then 'shocked' by flooding in magenta dye

Using the Leftovers

The key aim here is to "waste not, want not" and find surprising colours and colour schemes. Remember that as there's no soda in your dye solutions they'll last for about 3 days so you can always explore using leftovers at a later stage.

Using young, still-warm leftover dyes
- Soda-soak and arrange your cloth as you want it in a tray.
- Apply the fresh, still-warm leftover dyes in a very random manner until the cloth is saturated.
- Leave over-night.
- In the morning, carefully drain the dregs into the sink, leaving the tray with as little dye solution in it as you can.
- Now mix a 'shocking' colour (try black or magenta) and apply this colour sparingly over the surface of the cloth so that it only hits the top of the pleats/folds/scrumples. Think accents.
- Leave for a minimum of 4 hours then rinse and wash as usual.

Using old, cold leftover dyes
- Soda-soak and arrange your cloth as you want it in a tray.
- Consider combining the left-over dye colours to make secondaries or complex colours.
- Whether using the dye solutions on their own or mixing them, wake them up by adding some hot water.
- Now apply all of the leftover colours across the cloth in any kind of manner. Blend by massaging the cloth where the colours meet to avoid hard edges.
- Now mix a new, medium-strength colour and either apply it to the surface of the cloth to add areas of accent or pattern, or flood the tray from the bottom.
- Let the tray sit for a minimum of 4 hours, then rinse and wash.

Leftover Soup
Leftover Soup is basically free-spirited bucket dyeing (a more considered approach is covered in the next section!).

- Put 3 to 6 tablespoons of soda ash into a bucket and dissolve with 1 to 2 litres of warm water.
- Throw all of the leftover dyes into the soda mixture and if necessary, add more hot water to raise the level of the vat (which will also wake up old, cold dyes).
- Consider the dye strength you might have (a wild guess is fine) and estimate how much meterage you could dye. Throw it into the bucket and stir for 5 minutes. (Note; for a stronger colour, use less cloth. For a paler colour, use more cloth.).
- Put some water in another bucket and place it on top of the dye bucket. This will ensure the cloth is below the level of dye solution to avoid unsightly air bubble marks.
- Leave at least 12 hours/overnight, then rinse and wash as usual.

Leftover soup can generate fantastic complex colours that are suitable for discharge work, more tray dyeing, over-dyeing, fabric paints etc.

You can get fabulous cloth from Leftover Soup!

Tray Dyeing | 37

Cloth that has been tray-dyed three times and bucket over-dyed once

Spring growth in the woods

Over-Dyeing for Richness & Depth

1st tray-dye; the key elements of texture are in

2nd tray-dye; more texture now, and more colour

3rd tray-dye; voilà – trees!

Right at the beginning we stated that we never expect to get the perfect piece of cloth from a single process. Sometimes this can happen but more often than not, several processes are needed to create cloth that has real depth and is rich in colour and texture.

At times you'll get exactly what you want from a single tray dye but we encourage you to tray-dye a piece of cloth more than once, or tray-dye it and then over-dye it in a bucket. Dyeing a piece of cloth twice using the tray method gives you the opportunity to further explore colour and generate additional texture at the same time. Over-dyeing in the bucket enables you to see how a new colour effects the ones already present in the cloth.

Over-Dyeing in the Tray

There are many ways forward when you tray-dye a piece of cloth for the second time. To avoid complete chaos, arrange the cloth in the same manner as you did the first time around (e.g. scrumple, pleat or spiral but don't mix methods).

Here are some variables to contemplate and when you consider how to apply the dyes this second time around - remember you can baste directly on to the surface of the cloth, or flood the tray from the bottom (or both).

- Cold-to-Warm or Warm-to-Cold; if your first tray-dye used a warm primary (or primaries), tray-dye the second time around using cold colour(s).
- Secondaries; what effect would over-dyeing in a secondary have?
- Complementaries; what would happen if you used a complementary colour on the cloth you're about to over-dye?
- Complex or 'murked-up' colour(s); what impact would a complex or murked-up colour have if you used it for the second tray-dye?
- Black or Brown; would using black or brown as the over-dye colour make the colours already in your cloth richer? How would they alter the basic colour scheme?
- Playing with dye strengths; try altering the strength of the over-dye colour(s) by making them weaker or stronger than the first colour(s) used on the cloth. Flooding a new, strong-strength dye colour across the bottom of the tray can often produce very exciting results.

Your choices are almost unlimited, which is both exciting and scary. The only way you'll learn is to get on with it!

The top half of the pictures shows the result of the tray-dye. The bottom half shows what happened to the cloth after it was over-dyed in the bucket with Magenta

Over-Dyeing in the Bucket

The key difference between over-dyeing in the tray and over-dyeing in the bucket is one of texture. Bucket or high-water immersion dyeing is an approach that generally seeks a smoother, more even finish to the cloth and as such, uses more water. Stirring is also a key element in achieving a smoother finish as it encourages the dye molecules to float around and find their way in to the cloth in a more even manner.

So why over-dye in the bucket? Quite simply, at times you'll want to change the colours or deepen what's already there without generating competing texture.

With tray-dyeing, the dye solutions are directly applied on to the surface of the cloth. When bucket dyeing, they float around and find their own way in. As such we prefer to use a slightly different recipe to the one we've been using for tray-dyeing. The dye amounts are more variable, the salt proportions to dye amounts are slightly different and more water is involved. Read on - but if using a different recipe for bucket-dyeing is likely to confuse you, simply use the recipe you've been using for tray-dyeing (see page 18) – it'll still generate good results.

Recipe for Bucket/High Water Immersion Dyeing

The amounts shown in each row are sufficient for 1 metre of standard-weight cotton.

The amount of dye and salt solution used will affect the end result in terms of the depth of colour. So;

- for fine-weight fabrics (particularly silks) mix at the lower end of each spectrum
- for heavier-weight, sturdy fabrics, mix at the upper end of each spectrum.

Dye Amounts	Salt Solution
2 to 3 teaspoons of dye	1 litre of strong (200ml salt) salt solution, warm-to-hot
1 to 2 teaspoons of dye	750ml strong salt solution (a 3/4 portion)
1/2 to 1 teaspoon of dye	500ml of strong salt solution (a 1/2 portion)
1/8 to 1/2 teaspoon of dye	250ml of strong salt solution (a 1/4 portion)

In addition, alter the recipe proportionately by reducing or increasing the dye & salt quantities for smaller amounts of cloth.

Over-dyeing tray-dyed cloth in the bucket

The dye solution is mixed as follows;

- Put some warm water in a mixing beaker and measure in the amount of dye you require. Stir well and if you're having problems getting the dye to dissolve, transfer the dye to a lidded container and shake vigorously (consider adding a teaspoon of Urea if you're having trouble). Top up with more warm water and stir again.
- Now measure out the appropriate amount of strong salt solution and put it in to a bucket (doesn't matter if it's cold).
- Add some warm water to this bucket and add 3 tablespoons of soda ash (6 tablespoons if using more than 3 teaspoons of dye). Stir well to dissolve.
- Put the dye solution into the bucket and stir to distribute.
- Now add more warm-to-hot water to bring up the level of the 'bath' – say one third to half full for 1 to 2 metres of cloth. Remember – the level of water won't affect the dye strength. If you've used the right amount of salt and dye to achieve the depth of colour on the meterage you want, adding water to the bath (coupled with stirring) will simply help you to generate a more even, smooth finish that won't compete with the texture you already have on the cloth.
- Place your cloth in the bucket (there's no need to soda-soak it first as the soda-ash is in already in the solution).
- Stir the vat well for 5 minutes to begin with and then stir every 30 minutes across a 4-hour period, or longer. (If you can't resist going for more texture, stir less frequently, or not at all after the cloth has been added).
- Whilst the vat is sitting, put some water in another bucket and place it on top of the dye vat. This will ensure the cloth is below the level of dye solution to avoid unsightly air bubble marks.
- Rinse as described on page 26.

And remember, what colour you choose to use for over-dyeing in the bucket is up to you – explore some of the suggestions given on page 37.

Trouble Shooting

At times you'll be less than pleased with your results so we thought it might be helpful to provide a list of key things to consider when striving to develop yourself.

I'm getting weak, feeble colours

- Are you 100% sure your cloth is made from natural fibres? (Silk, cotton, hemp, linen or viscose/rayon)
- Was it scoured to remove size? (We always scour linen and hemp even if it's sold prepared for dyeing)
- Did you use your cloth dry? (if so, the dyes may have found it hard to penetrate)
- Did you soda soak your cloth for long enough and if so, is the soda ash/sodium carbonate you're using 100% pure?
- Did you use strong enough dyes for the type of cloth you used, and did you put enough on to the cloth?
- Was your dye solution warm enough?
- When applying the dyes, did you work slowly and steadily, ensuring they penetrated the cloth all the way to the bottom of the tray?
- Did you leave your tray-dye to fix for at least 4 hours?

I'm getting muddy or indistinct colours

Ask yourself the questions listed above and then ask yourself some more;

- Was your cloth too loosely arranged? (if so, the dye solutions will have found it easy to mix and mingle).
- Did you massage and meddle with the arranged cloth (too much) once the dyes had been applied?
- What's the quality of your cloth? (e.g. poor quality such as loomstate).
- Is one colour of dye over-whelming the results?

There's too much white in my cloth

- How tightly packed was your cloth? (Very tight compaction will make it harder for the dyes to penetrate down)
- When applying the dyes, did you work slowly and steadily, ensuring they penetrated the cloth all the way to the bottom of the tray?
- Did you massage the cloth, or press it down (as you worked or 15 minutes later)?

The texture/marks aren't strong enough

- How well did you arrange the cloth?
- Was it soda-soaked?
- How wet was it when you arranged it? (Wetter cloth will generate more subtle textural marks).
- Was it well compacted? (Too loose means less crisp texture/marks).
- When applying the dyes, did you work slowly and steadily, ensuring they penetrated the cloth all the way to the bottom of the tray?
- Did your tray have plenty of dye sitting in the bottom of it once you'd finished applying them? (If not, you didn't apply enough).
- When applying the dyes, did you consider the way in which you were doing it? (Perhaps you used two close colours side-by-side, perhaps the arrangement of the colours was too even).
- Did you massage the cloth, or press it down (as you worked or 15 minutes later)?
- Did you consider flooding the bottom of the tray to create additional texture?

If you've got 'dogs' (which we all generate from time to time); re-dye them in the tray or over-dye them in the bucket.

And above all ask yourself; "how many times have I tried tray-dyeing?" Remember that it takes practise to achieve mastery…

Resources/Suppliers

The website (www.committedtocloth.com) has a list of suppliers, but the following companies will be able to provide you with what you need. Remember, if it's a web-based company, many ship worldwide.

EUROPE

Ario
5 Pengry Road, Loughor, Swansea SA4 6PH
www.ario.co.uk

Art Van Go
The Studios, 1 Stevenage Road, Knebworth, Herts G3 6AN
www.artvango.co.uk

The Bramble Patch
West Street, Weedon, Northamptonshire NN7 4QU
www.thebramblepatch.co.uk

Fibrecrafts/George Weil
Old Portsmouth Road, Peasmarsh, Guildford, Surrey GU3 1LZ
www.fibrecrafts.co.uk

Nannas Verksted
Skolebakken 29, 1628 Engelsviken, Norway
www.nannasverksted.no

Quiltstar (also provides a thermofax service)
Schnewlinstr. 5a, 79098 Freiberg, Germany
www.quiltstar.de

Quilt und Textile
Sebastiansplatz 4, Muncih 80331, Germany
www.quiltundtextilkunst.de

Patchwork Shop(also provides a thermofax service)
www.patchworkshop.de or www.pdpm.de

Spektrum Textil
Radhusvej 2, 2920 Charlottenlund, Copenhagen, Denmark
www.spektrumtextil.dk

Stone Creek Silk (incorporating Thermofax-Online)
Stone Creek House, Sunk Island, East Yorkshire, HU12 0AP
www.stonecreeksilk.co.uk

Thermofax Screens
Foxley Farm, Foxley, Towcester NN12 8HP
www.thermofaxscreens.co.uk

Whaleys
Harris Court, Great Horton, Bradford, West Yorkshire
www.whaleys-bradford.ltd.uk

Winifred Cottage
17 Elms Road, Fleet, Hampshire GU51 3EG
www.winifredcottage.co.uk

Zijdelings
Kapelstraat 93a, 5046 CL Tilberg, The Netherlands
www.zijdelings.com

NORTH AMERICA

Dharma Trading Company (U.S.A.)
1604 Fourth Street, San Rafael, California 94901
www.dharmatrading.com

GS Dye (Canada)
250 Dundas Street West, No. 8, Toronto M5T 2Z5, Ontario
www.gsdye.com

Maiwa (Canada)
6-1666 Johnston Street, Granville Island, Vancouver V6H 3SZ, B.C.
Maiwa.com

ProChemical & Dye (U.S.A.)
PO Box 14, Somerset, MA 02726
www.prochemical.com

Rupert, Gibbon & Spider (U.S.A.)
PO Box 452, Healdsburg, CA 95448
www.jacquardproducts.com

NEW ZEALAND & AUSTRALIA

Artbeat of Tasmania (Tasmania, Australia)
85 Channel Highway, Kingston, Tasmania 7050
www.artbeattas.com

Artisan Books (Australia)
159 Gertrude St, Fitzroy 3065, Victoria
www.artisan.com.au

Batik Oetoro (Australia)
8/9 Arnhem Close, Gateshead, NSW 2290
www.dyeman.com

Essential Textile Art (Australia)
PO Box 3416, Rundle Mall, SA 5000
www.essentialtextileart.com

KraftKolour (Australia)
Box 379, Whittlesea, Victoria 3757
www.kraftkolour.com.au

New Zealand Quilter (New Zealand)
PO Box 14567, Kilbirnie, Wellington 6241
www.nzquilter.co.nz

The Thread Studio (Australia)
6 Smith Street, Perth 6000
www.thethreadstudio.com